A CREATIVE JOURNAL

THE

5-MINUTE BIBLE STUDY MAP FOR MEN

BARBOUR PUBLISHING

Print ISBN 979-8-89151-185-9

Published by Barbour Publishing, Inc., 1810 Barbour Drive, Uhrichsville, Ohio 44683, www.barbourbooks.com

Our mission is to inspire the world with the life-changing message of the Bible.

Member of the Evangelical Christian Publishers Association

Printed in China.

FOLLOW THE MAP TO KNOW GOD AND HIS WORD MORE!

This fantastic Bible study journal provides an avenue for you to open God's Word regularly and dig in to a passage—even if you have only five minutes!

Minutes 1–2: ***Read*** carefully the scripture passage for each day's Bible study.

Minute 3: ***Understand.*** Read a brief devotional based on the day's scripture.

Minute 4: ***Apply.*** Answer the questions designed to help you apply the verses from the Bible to your own life.

Minute 5: ***Pray.*** A dedicated spot for prayer will allow you to talk to God about anything on your mind.

May *The 5-Minute Bible Study Map for Men* help you establish the discipline of studying God's Word. You will find that spending even five minutes focused on scripture and prayer has the power to make a huge difference. Soon you will want to make room for even more time in God's Word!

DATE: ....

JESUS CAN SATISFY YOUR DESIRES

READ JOHN 6:25–40

UNDERSTAND

Why are you following Jesus? It's a question many of His earliest followers had to confront. In today's scripture reading, people sought Him for a steady supply of food so that they would never go hungry again. Although that's an understandable motivation at a time of Roman oppression (with droughts and famines sometimes making things worse) Jesus wanted them to know they were missing the bigger point of His ministry.

Jesus asks you to consider what you crave today. Examine your desires and consider whether they are drawing you closer to Him. It's possible that you crave something other than what Jesus offers. So do you truly believe that Jesus can give you something better?

The manna God provided in the desert sustained the people of Israel physically, but Jesus, the bread of life, offers to sustain you spiritually, leading you to a place of peace and restoration. Jesus is with you, and much like a loaf of bread dropping from the sky into your lap, His Spirit has come to you so that He can be fully present with you.

....

....

....

....

....

....

....

APPLY

How does Jesus' use of physical needs (food) help people understand their need for Him?

What do you think the people talking with Jesus really wanted from Him?

PRAY

DATE: ....

THE GOD WHO WANTS TO KNOW YOU

READ ACTS 17:22–31

UNDERSTAND

The goal of religion is to tell us how we can find God. But Christianity comes at it the opposite way, revealing a God who comes to find us. His approach goes against our nature. Our default setting is self-sufficiency: We want to save ourselves and be free to determine our own purpose.

Even so, we grasp intuitively that things aren't the way they should be. The world is broken and unfixable, at least by us. Jesus is the fixer of all that is wrong with us and the world, and He wants to know you personally.

In Acts 17, Paul made it clear that the God the Greeks called "Unknown" is actually the God who made everything, who is bigger than any set of beliefs, any idol, or any philosophy. And He is closer than we think, bestowing His common grace according to His good will to the "just and unjust alike" (Matthew 5:45 NLT). He is a God of action and progress.

God's strange and wonderful purposes are fully displayed in Jesus Christ—God made flesh. He came to meet His own standards of righteousness and judgment, conquering the grave and sin so we could know Him personally. If that doesn't change the game for you, God remains unknown.

....

....

....

....

....

APPLY

How has God made Himself known to you?

In what areas do you tend to slip back into self-sufficiency instead of relying on God?

PRAY

DATE: ....

FIRST THOUGHTS

READ PSALM 5:1–3

UNDERSTAND

Even if you're not a morning person, it's still a good idea to focus on God first thing. It doesn't have to be a full-on study (especially if you're no good pre-coffee). Just talk to God as soon as you can. A psalm of praise is a great way to offer God your first thoughts.

It helps to do a little prep work the night before. Find a Bible verse or passage you want to focus on, then bookmark it so you can grab it the next morning and read it to God. You can read the verse as a prayer or use it as a launching pad for what comes to mind.

Then, spend a few moments in silence, just to see if God impresses anything on your heart—a thought that you're reasonably sure came from Him and not you, a word of challenge or awareness, or even just a sense that it's good to seek God.

You can even do the same passage several days in a row to help fasten it onto your memory and into your heart. As a bonus, watch for ways that God will repeat and confirm what you've read during the day or the week. He has His ways of letting you know His eye is on you and He sees what you're doing in faith each morning.

....

....

....

....

....

....

....

....

APPLY

How often do you praise God simply for being who He is?

How does the thought of God waiting to hear from you in the morning make you feel?

PRAY

DATE: ....

FAITH OVERCOMES FEAR

READ NEHEMIAH 4:11–20

UNDERSTAND

In times of uncertainty, even threats to your well-being, the words of Nehemiah cut through the challenges: "Remember the Lord, who is great and awesome" (Nehemiah 4:14 NIV). It's possible to lose perspective and forget who or what is great, awesome, or powerful. You may even feel like your afflictions are greater than God's power and presence.

Feelings of fear aren't unusual even for the man of God, but how we respond to fear and uncertainty will make all the difference.

Consider how Nehemiah sought to remind the people of God's power and helped them get back to the work at hand—even if they had to carry weapons while on the job. The people kept working on what God had called them to do, but first they addressed the spiritual and physical elements of their situation.

Afflictions and opposition will come, but that doesn't mean that the Lord has abandoned you. Such difficulties are opportunities for you to rely more completely on God's power and to examine the role of faith in your life. Through living by faith and trusting in God, you'll overcome fear, knowing that the Lord is with you.

....

....

....

....

....

....

....

APPLY

How did Nehemiah respond to the people's fear?

Why did Nehemiah give God the credit for frustrating their enemies' plans?

PRAY

DATE: ....

IS YOUR HEART FULLY COMMITTED TO GOD?

READ 2 CHRONICLES 16:7–14

UNDERSTAND

If you'd like to become better able to confront the challenges you face today, the best course you can take is to address the state of your heart. What is your heart fully committed to right now? Answering that question can help you make an honest assessment of your spiritual state and whether God will be present to strengthen you.

If you persist in going your own way and relying on your own strength and plans, you can expect to be disappointed, even devastated. At some point either you will need to double down on your own ways (and accept the consequences they bring) or confess your failures. It may be painful to confess the ways you've gone astray, but the sooner you turn back to the Lord, the sooner you'll be back on track with Him.

Even better, the Lord is looking for you to turn back to Him. You don't have to work to get God's attention or act in a certain way. Once you've shifted the orientation of your heart, you'll be ready for His loving gaze, which is already turned your way.

....

....

....

....

....

....

....

....

APPLY

What were the consequences of Asa relying on his own plans to solve his problems?

How could Asa have responded more constructively to the prophet's message?

PRAY

DATE: ....

LEAVE JUDGMENT TO GOD

READ 1 CORINTHIANS 4:1–13

UNDERSTAND

Although it's helpful to assess yourself, to evaluate your motives, and to listen to the advice of people you trust, Paul cautioned that these measures aren't the very best approach. In fact, escaping the scrutiny of humans is hardly proof of innocence.

It is far more useful to examine your conscience before God and to seek to prove yourself before Him. There is nothing you can hide from God, and so you can believe that God's judgment will be true and just.

If thoughts of God's judgment leave you unsettled, just remember that you can trust in His willingness to forgive your sins and to wipe them away when you repent. When you come clean with God, you can be assured that you are free from judgment and don't have to live in uncertainty. Even better, when God's Spirit guides you, you will live in the freedom and peace Jesus promised His followers. That doesn't mean you'll be free from conflict an misunderstanding—Paul himself was no stranger to conflict-induced assumptions, judgment, and second-guessing arising in the churches he founded—but in the Spirit, you'll see the way forward.

....

....

....

....

....

....

....

APPLY

Why would Paul leave judgment to God alone?

What are the benefits of waiting for God's judgment on yourself or someone else?

PRAY

DATE: ....

HOPE IN THE DARKNESS

READ LUKE 22:39–46

UNDERSTAND

At Gethsemane, Jesus looked down the barrel of God's wrath, the first and only time in His eternal existence that He would be separated from the perfect community of the Trinity. He faced a darkness that we as Christians will never have to—the eternal, dissolving misery of getting what we deserve as sinners.

And right before that unbearable event, Jesus couldn't even get His closest friends to pray with Him. Another would turn Him over to the authorities, and the crowds that lined His path with palm fronds a week earlier would be calling for His execution in a few hours.

If your heart aches thinking about that, let it ache. But then take comfort in knowing that Jesus understands darkness. Just as God sent an angel to comfort and strengthen Him, He will send comfort to you too in your darkest hours.

God asks us to do hard things at times and allows trials and troubles into our lives—not always because we've sinned but because He wants us to seek Him no matter what, to share in Christ's sufferings, and then to be strengthened with the hope He bought with His blood. The separation from God we may feel is never actual distance. Jesus made sure of that.

....

....

....

....

....

....

APPLY

What is the hardest moment God has ever allowed you to face?

How did He eventually bring you comfort?

PRAY

DATE: ....

NEVER, NEVER GIVE UP

READ PSALM 27:7–14

UNDERSTAND

People bail on Jesus when the going gets tough. It was true two thousand years ago, and it's true today. When He doesn't meet our expectations, we often look for a savior who matches our expectations. At one point, in John 6:67–69 (ESV), Jesus even asked the Twelve if they were leaving Him too, and Peter said, "Lord, to whom shall we go? You have the words of eternal life, and we have believed. . . that you are the Holy One of God."

Centuries before, David saw the evil and cruelty in the world, recalled what he knew about God, and determined there was no one else worth trusting. He looked ahead to God's goodness in "the land of the living" (verse 13 ESV)—to the Messiah—and decided He was worth waiting on.

Knowing that God is working, even if it's behind the scenes, provides an anchor, a hope for those who believe. God never wastes pain. Every hardship, trial, and tear has purpose and meaning. The Bible lauds those who look beyond their immediate environment and trust in a kingdom yet to come—a creation restored and ruled with justice and compassion by the one who made it and then redeemed it. Don't lose heart. He is coming back, and He is here now, in the land of the living.

....

....

....

....

....

....

APPLY

How do you feel when it seems like God is not answering your prayers?

How do you usually look for God to work—in big ways or small ones?

PRAY

DATE: ....

LOVE LEADS TO GENEROSITY

READ 1 JOHN 3

UNDERSTAND

The crux of John's first epistle is God's love for you. If you are aware of and have received that love, John wrote, then your life should be changed, different from what it was before. John gave the example of Jesus as both the *proof* of just how deep God's love is for you and the *example* of how to love others sacrificially. When you have the foundation of God's love built up within, you can then more fully express love and generosity to others.

John expected us to follow Jesus' example and lay down our own needs and desires for others. He used the example of financial generosity to make that point. Christians should be aware of the needs of others, and when they are, the love of God will compel them to meet those needs. This type of concern for others is evidence that you have truly been touched by God's love.

Your actions serve as the ultimate clue that you have received and been transformed by God's love. If you find yourself consumed with yourself, seek God and experience His love for you. Let the Lord transform you from the inside, and then the loving acts for others will follow.

....

....

....

....

....

....

....

APPLY

How did John want his readers to apply Jesus' example to their own lives?

What does today's passage say about how Christians should treat one another?

PRAY

DATE:..

SEEK TO SERVE GOD ABOVE ALL ELSE

READ 2 TIMOTHY 2:1–13

UNDERSTAND

The goals of a soldier or athlete are clear and simple. Soldiers obey their commanders, and athletes channel all their energy toward competing for first place. A half measure or divided priorities simply won't work. You're either "all in" as a soldier or an athlete, or you're ineffectively divided in your commitments.

Paul gave Timothy reminders about his simple gospel message: "Jesus Christ, raised from the dead, descended from David" (2 Timothy 2:8 NIV). Jesus is alive, the fulfillment of God's promise to raise up a descendant of David to rule with justice and peace. No other person on earth is worthy of our allegiance, and no one else is as intimately aware of us.

Moments of suffering can truly test your commitments and even send you off track with your goals. Suffering may prompt you to look for the easy way out or tempt you to give up. There may not appear to be any point in enduring any longer. Yet, if your goal is to win the prize of intimacy with God, then there's no question about enduring hardships. You may have to push yourself beyond what you think your limits are, but if you persevere to the end, no one can take away God's reward for you.

....

....

....

....

....

APPLY

What are the requirements of a soldier, and how did Paul apply them to Christians?

Why is it so important for Christians to endure suffering?

PRAY

DATE: ....

WHOM DO YOU TRUST?

READ JEREMIAH 17:5–12

UNDERSTAND

What you trust in goes a long way toward determining the amount of turbulence and turmoil in your life. You could trust in money or in powerful relationships, but both could disappear in an instant; they are very much at the mercy of life's circumstances. Ecclesiastes speaks of this approach to the world as a "chasing after the wind" (NIV). There is no foundation and no place to go for security when you trust in the unreliable resources of this world.

By contrast, trusting in the Lord leads to stability, new life, and flourishing. Whether life is difficult or humming along according to plan, you can find a measure of peace and rest by relying on the Lord to direct your paths and to provide what you need. By growing in this trust, you can see your worries and fears fade away.

Besides the benefits you enjoy today by trusting in the Lord, you'll also be rewarded by God according to what you do. God is tuned in to what you're thinking and doing, and if you can live from a foundation of trust in the Lord, you can also look forward to the next life with hope and peace.

....

....

....

....

....

....

....

....

APPLY

What do you need to entrust to the Lord today?

How does trusting fully in the Lord help you bear spiritual fruit?

PRAY

DATE: ....

SEEKING THE RIGHT THING

READ MATTHEW 6:24–34

UNDERSTAND

Jesus goes straight to the root of money's powerful entanglement, and His approach offers you freedom. . .if you're willing to ask some difficult questions. His probing question "Why do you have so little faith?" addresses the need everyone feels for security and the struggle to trust God with it. Money simply becomes a path toward security, making it possible to eat, to wear nice-looking clothes, and to live secure in a safe home.

The good news is that God knows what you need, and He has much compassion for you as you weigh the burdens of providing for yourself and others. He never leaves you alone, and Jesus assures you that relying on God's provision will pay off.

Relying on money for security can truly backfire, as it can become a cruel master. You will always wonder if you have enough, and your faith in money will replace your faith in God. You can have money while placing your faith in God, but you should always rely on Him, not money, as your source of security.

....

....

....

....

....

....

....

....

APPLY

How does worrying about your needs reveal what you're pursuing?

How could Matthew 6:24–34 impact the way you pray about your daily needs?

PRAY

DATE: ....

WHO'S PURSUING WHOM?

READ JOHN 6:41–45

UNDERSTAND

We tend to pursue God the way we start a hobby. We do the choosing—the activity, time, and place—and think we'll get better at being Christians if we just work at it. But before we can do anything for God, we need to understand that we wouldn't even care about God if He didn't care about us first.

God is all-powerful, all-knowing, and omnipresent. He gave up something very precious to Him so we might someday understand and respond to His initiative. He enables our goodness and fixes our brokenness. With great acts of power, mercy, and love, He draws us to Himself.

Pursuing God starts by acknowledging that He is the original pursuer. It's His overwhelming, all-in love we respond to when we say we're pursuing Him. As 1 John 4:19 (NKJV) notes, "We love Him because He first loved us."

The pursuit of God is comforting and challenging, calming and confounding. But that's God. He is both loving Father and holy Lord of all—closer than a brother and harder to grasp than quantum physics. God sacrificed His precious Son to save you, which imparts both terrible news (you're that much of a sinner) and great news (He thinks you're worth dying for).

....

....

....

....

....

....

APPLY

What led you to commit your life to follow Christ?

How was God working in your life leading up to that moment?

PRAY

DATE: ....

THE BEST FASTING BENEFITS OTHERS

READ ISAIAH 58

UNDERSTAND

There is certainly a place for practices such as fasting and humbling yourself before God in prayer, but in today's scripture reading, the prophet Isaiah told God's people to never substitute those practices for dealing with injustice, oppression, and the needs of others. God is far more concerned with how you treat others than with how you worship.

In a way, caring for others *is* a kind of worship. If you want to demonstrate your commitment to God, care for others in the same way He cares for you. When you have an abundance or extra resources, share them with others so that they can benefit from the blessings you've received.

The result of this kind of worship is that God will hear your prayers and honor them. If you are generous with others, God will be generous with you. In fact, you will find new dimensions of joy in God as you enter into the kind of life that God imagines for His people.

....

....

....

....

....

....

....

....

APPLY

What is the condition God gives for acknowledging His people's prayers?

How could this passage change the way you worship God this week?

PRAY

DATE: ....

TRUE PURPOSE

READ EPHESIANS 2:1–10

UNDERSTAND

The Greek word Paul used in Ephesians 2:10 for workmanship is *poiema*, meaning "something made." We get our English words *poem* and *poetry* from it. Paul used it one other time, in Romans 1:20 (ESV), when he noted that God's "invisible attributes, namely, his eternal power and divine nature, have been clearly perceived, ever since the creation of the world, in the things that have been made."

When God created the world, He poured His eternal power and divine nature into all He made and called it good. You are an example of His finest work—the reason some translations of Ephesians 2:10 replace *workmanship* with *masterpiece*. Not only is God shaping and crafting you into a unique expression of His love and power, but He is brimming with purpose for you.

We are used to thinking of art as a result—a painting, a statue, a composition in words or music—that expresses something about the artist. If God is the artist, the way He is sculpting you can result only in more than you can dream or imagine. You matter to your maker. Nothing and no one can fulfill you like He can, and no one can delight Him the way you do. Listen for His calling, do everything for His glory, and enjoy all He has for you.

....

....

....

....

....

....

APPLY

How would you describe your purpose?

How quick are you to follow God's leading? What holds you back?

PRAY

DATE: ....

BEING FULLY KNOWN

READ PSALM 139:1–6

UNDERSTAND

God has perfect knowledge of every subject the human mind can consider, plus far more that we can't. No one teaches God anything; He has nothing to learn and is never surprised. All the folks who think they will have questions for God when they see Him are in for a rude awakening. The superiority of His knowledge beggars the answers they think He owes them.

God knows everything about you. He knows the ways you're different on Sunday morning than on Friday night. He knows when your thoughts wander, and where. You can protest what feels like an invasion of privacy, but He knows exactly what you're going to say.

We're contradictory creatures. We hate when people use information about us against us, yet we long to be known and understood by someone who is truly for us. When David wrote in Psalm 139:5 (NKJV), "You have hedged me behind and before, and laid Your hand upon me," he was squirming beneath the weight of God's omniscience, probably because he realized that all his comings and goings—every thought, word, and deed—weren't always pleasing to God.

God knows everything about you and still thinks you were worth dying for. He knows both who you are and who you are becoming in Christ—someone like Jesus, someone beyond your wildest dreams.

....

....

....

....

....

APPLY

How does the fact that God knows everything affect your decision-making?

When was the last time you thought you knew better than God?

PRAY

DATE: ....

THE EDGY COMFORT OF GOD'S OMNIPRESENCE

READ PSALM 139:7–12

UNDERSTAND

God knows everything and is present in every place and moment. Does that comfort you or make you nervous? A little tension is good for any relationship—keeping us from taking the other person for granted—but especially with God. We cannot limit Him, nor can we fully understand Him.

In Psalm 139:6 (NLT), David described God's omniscience as "too great for me to understand." He realized there was nowhere he could go where God was not. God is equally and fully present in both light and darkness. We cannot escape accountability to God. The end of this life is the beginning of eternity.

Even for believers, that creates friction. Where is God in our suffering? We take comfort in a Romans 8:28 sense, knowing it's God's specialty to work good things out of bad. But we also know that God demands total control over our entire life. And man, is giving everything over to Him a process!

The Christian life is built on the belief that suffering has value and purpose in God's good hands. We are saved from hell but still challenged by our flesh, the world, and the devil. But even in our darkest hours, we are not hidden from Him. He is making all things right.

....

....

....

....

....

APPLY

When was the last time you behaved as if God couldn't see you?

When was the last time God comforted you in a hard moment?

PRAY

DATE: ....

ABUNDANT LIFE IS SIMPLE

READ JOHN 15:1–11

UNDERSTAND

Every follower of Jesus bears a measure of responsibility for their choices and actions, but Jesus makes it abundantly clear that you are not solely responsible for producing spiritual growth. Any changes in your life or growth in your spiritual awareness of God comes directly from Jesus. Any benefits that others enjoy because of your abundant life in God can be traced to Jesus' intervention in your life, not your own efforts or willpower.

Jesus invites you to walk a fine line where you must choose to remain in Him. There is a decision and an action in this. If you don't remain in Him, you will surely wither. But if you choose to remain in Him and put in the effort to keep Him at the forefront of your life, He will produce the life of God in you.

Jesus keeps it simple, telling His followers to cultivate a life of faith and dependence on Him. Once you are united with Him, your desires will begin to line up with His, and prayer will become much simpler because you won't have to worry about what to seek from God. The starting point is determining how you can ensure that you are abiding in Jesus today and every day.

....

....

....

....

....

....

....

APPLY

What kinds of spiritual practices can you do to remain in Jesus?

How can you prevent being apart from Jesus?

PRAY

DATE: ....

THE REAL WAKE-UP CALL

READ PSALM 139:13–18

UNDERSTAND

God's unmatched power saturates your life, from the moment of your conception through the moment of your death and into eternity. In Psalm 139:13–16, David praised the Lord's hand in creating his life in such an awe-inspiring fashion. God's great power works on the most personal level—the wonders of the cell, of pregnancy, of His knowing exactly how long each of us will live. Then David topped it off: "When I awake, I am still with You" (verse 18 NKJV). He was talking about more than a good night's rest.

Sleep is often a biblical metaphor for both physical and spiritual death. For the Christian, then, to wake up is to step into new life—salvation in this life and eternity with Christ after death. In some sense, David understood that death wasn't the final separation from God but a crossing of the threshold into eternal life with Him.

In Psalm 17:15 (NLT), David anticipated that moment: "Because I am righteous, I will see you. When I awake, I will see you face to face and be satisfied." We do the best we can and trust God to make sense of all the hard, broken things in this life. When we die, we will wake up to all that God has for us in eternity and be satisfied.

....

....

....

....

....

....

....

APPLY

How does God use His power on your behalf?

How does God's promise never to leave you affect your daily life?

PRAY

DATE: ....

JESUS CARES FOR YOUR WELL-BEING

READ JOHN 10:1–15

UNDERSTAND

As a follower of Jesus, you are His sheep and He is your loving shepherd. Being a part of Jesus' flock means that you follow Him and that He cares for you and protects you. In fact, Jesus is so committed to your well-being and safety that He was willing to lay down His life for you. Jesus doesn't lead you and protect you because of what He can gain for Himself—He leads and protects because He is genuinely committed to your safety and thriving.

There may have been moments in your life when someone who should have cared for you didn't, preferring to place their own interests ahead of yours. But in the safety of Jesus' presence, you won't be neglected or discarded.

Jesus wants you to listen for His voice and to respond to it. There are many different ways to be attentive to Jesus' voice. You may be especially attuned to Him when you read scripture each day, or you may wait on the Lord in silent but hopeful expectation as you pray. However you listen for God's direction in your life, He will show up to lead you forward in very much the same way an earthly shepherd leads his sheep.

....

....

....

....

....

....